OKLAHOMA STATE
COWBOYS

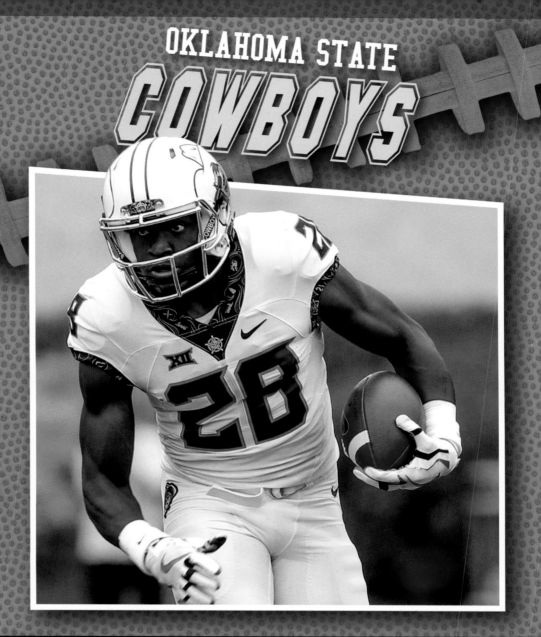

BY THOMAS CAROTHERS

SportsZone

An Imprint of Abdo Publishing
abdopublishing.com

abdopublishing.com

Published by Abdo Publishing, a division of ABDO, PO Box 398166, Minneapolis, Minnesota 55439.
Copyright © 2019 by Abdo Consulting Group, Inc. International copyrights reserved in all countries.
No part of this book may be reproduced in any form without written permission from the publisher.
SportsZone™ is a trademark and logo of Abdo Publishing.

Printed in the United States of America, North Mankato, Minnesota
032018
092018

Cover Photo: Frank Jansky/Icon Sportswire/AP Images
Interior Photos: Frank Jansky/Icon Sportswire/AP Images, 1; Charles Baus/Cal Sport Media/AP Images,
4–5; Ross D. Franklin/AP Images, 6, 11; Matt York/AP Images, 9; Ernest K. Bennet/AP Images, 12–13, 43
(top left); Carl Linde/AP Images, 15, 43 (top middle); AP Images, 18–19; David Stacy/Icon Sportswire/
AP Images, 20, 43 (bottom left); NFL Photos/AP Images, 23, 42; Rich Clarkson/Sports Illustrated/
Getty Images, 25; Dave Crenshaw/AP Images, 26–27; AP Images, 29; Itsuo Inouye/AP Images, 30; J.
Pat Carter/AP Images, 33; Nate Billings/The Oklahoman/AP Images, 34–35; Sue Ogrocki/AP Images,
37; Rogelio V. Solis/AP Images, 38; Phelan M. Ebenhack /AP Images, 41; AP Images, 43 (top right); Sue
Ogrocki/AP Images, 43 (bottom right); William Purnell/Icon Sportswire/AP Images, 44

Editor: Julie Dick
Series Designer: Craig Hinton

Library of Congress Control Number: 2017962092

Publisher's Cataloging-in-Publication Data

Names: Carothers, Thomas, author.
Title: Oklahoma State Cowboys / by Thomas Carothers.
Description: Minneapolis, Minnesota : Abdo Publishing, 2019. | Series: Inside college football | Includes
      online resources and index.
Identifiers: ISBN 9781532114595 (lib.bdg.) | ISBN 9781532154423 (ebook)
Subjects: LCSH: American football--Juvenile literature. | College sports--United States-- History-
      -Juvenile literature. | Oklahoma State Cowboys (Football team)--Juvenile literature. |
      Football--Records--United States--Juvenile literature.
Classification: DDC 796.332630--dc23

TABLE OF CONTENTS

Wide receiver Justin Blackmon received several awards while playing for the Cowboys.

FIESTA BOWL FIREWORKS

THE GREATEST SEASON IN OKLAHOMA STATE UNIVERSITY (OSU) HISTORY RESTED ON THE FOOT OF QUINN SHARP. THE COWBOYS' JUNIOR PLACEKICKER WAS LINING UP A 23-YARD FIELD GOAL TO WIN THE FIESTA BOWL ON JANUARY 2, 2012. ALL HE HAD TO DO WAS PUT THE BALL THROUGH THE UPRIGHTS.

The Fiesta Bowl was a game of heavyweights. Both the fourth-ranked Stanford Cardinals and third-ranked OSU entered the game with 11–1 records. Stanford's loss came at home against a strong Oregon team. The Cowboys' loss was much more painful.

OSU was ranked No. 2 in the country entering its game at Iowa State on November 18. But the Cowboys were playing with heavy hearts. Two OSU women's basketball coaches had died in a plane crash earlier that day. The Cowboys football team lost in double overtime, 37–31.

Despite the off-field tragedy and on-field setback of that day, the Cowboys finished the season strong. They drubbed rival Oklahoma 44–10. Winning the Fiesta Bowl would be a strong conclusion to the season.

Stanford's star player was quarterback Andrew Luck. He would later be the first pick in the National Football League (NFL) Draft. It would take every bit of Cowboy firepower to hang with Luck and the powerful Cardinal attack. The game started in the Cardinals' favor. Stanford had a 14–0 lead early in the second quarter.

But Luck wasn't the only future NFL player on the field. Cowboys quarterback Brandon Weeden and wide receiver Justin Blackmon would also be first-round draft picks. Weeden had set school season and career records for passing yards, completions, and touchdown passes. He and Blackmon didn't take it easy on Stanford. Weeden connected with Blackmon on touchdown passes of 43 and 67 yards, with Sharp completing extra points to tie the game 14–14.

The offenses continued to hold the upper hand all night. OSU kept pace but couldn't take the lead. A touchdown by Cowboys running back Joseph Randle and an extra point by Sharp tied the game 38–38 with just over two minutes left in the game.

BRANDON WEEDEN

Oklahoma City native Brandon Weeden took an indirect route to Cowboys football. In high school, Weeden earned All-State honors in both football and baseball. He was drafted by the New York Yankees in 2002 and decided to give baseball a shot. But after four years struggling in the minor leagues, Weeden headed back home to play football at OSU. The path to stardom wasn't exactly quick in football, either. After taking a redshirt year in 2007, he played in just one game in 2008 and three in 2009.

Finally Weeden was named the starting quarterback in 2010. The next year he broke several school single-season records, including passing yards (4,727), completed passes (409), and completion percentage (72.4). In 2012 the Cleveland Browns chose Weeden with the 22nd pick of the first round in the NFL Draft.

JUSTIN BLACKMON

Justin Blackmon played in 38 games for OSU from 2008 to 2011. He set the school record for average receptions in a game with 6.7. Through 2017 Blackmon ranked second in school history with 253 career receptions, 3,564 receiving yards, and 40 touchdowns. The Jacksonville Jaguars drafted Blackmon in 2012 as the fifth pick in the first round. He was the highest draft selection for a Cowboys player since Barry Sanders was drafted third overall in 1989.

Stanford made the most of the remaining time, driving down the field in eight plays. Freshman kicker Jordan Williamson had a chance to win it with a 35-yard field goal at the end of regulation time. But he missed, sending the game into overtime. Stanford missed another field goal early in overtime, giving the ball back to the Cowboys.

Weeden took the field for his final series as a college quarterback. On second down he threw to wide receiver Colton Chelf, who appeared to score the game-winning touchdown. However, the Cowboys' celebration was put on hold as officials reviewed the play. They had to make sure Chelf had reached the end zone before he was tackled.

It had been a long road to this point. The Cowboys had slowly climbed back from a losing record in the 1990s. Head coach Les Miles had led the team to three bowl appearances in four years in the early 2000s. When Miles left OSU in 2004, Mike Gundy was promoted from offensive coordinator to head coach.

Gundy was no stranger to Cowboys football. He'd played quarterback from 1986–89. Future NFL Hall of Fame running backs

Quinn Sharp was sent in for a field goal attempt in overtime at the Fiesta Bowl.

Barry Sanders and Thurman Thomas had been on the same team. The 1988 Cowboys finished with a 10–2 record. It would be more than 20 years before the Cowboys won 10 games in a season again. In 2010 Gundy led the Cowboys to an 11–2 record.

The Cowboys began the 2011 season ranked No. 9 and surged as high as No. 2 in early November before the upset loss at Iowa State. A 44–10 defeat of Oklahoma in the regular season finale ensured a No. 3 ranking in the last poll and a spot in the Fiesta Bowl. Now, after a dozen games and four-plus quarters against Stanford, the Cowboys were on the verge of completing the team's first 12-win season and earning its highest final ranking in the national polls.

The officials broke their huddle. The referee announced that Chelf had been stopped just short of the goal line. Rather than risking a fumble or interception, Gundy decided to send in Sharp to win the game. Sharp, the Big 12 Special Teams Player of the Year, had made 20 of 23 field goal attempts in the regular season. And he had connected on a 19-yard field goal in the third quarter, his only attempt in the game.

The ball was snapped. The hold was perfect. And Sharp booted the ball through the uprights for a 41–38 win. After the game, the head coach helped put the victory in perspective.

"I think that from coast to coast, people have a lot of respect for Oklahoma State football," Gundy said. He dedicated the win to the victims of the November plane crash.

Coach Mike Gundy hugs Shelley Budke, widow of OSU women's basketball coach Kurt Budke.

Upon taking over as head coach in 1929, Lynn "Pappy" Waldorf led Oklahoma State to its first sustained success.

2

HUMBLE BEGINNINGS

THE OKLAHOMA STATE COWBOYS HAVE CHANGED SCHOOL NAMES AND NICKNAMES SEVERAL TIMES OVER THE YEARS. TODAY'S COWBOYS HAVE BEEN A CORNERSTONE OF THE BIG 12 CONFERENCE FOR SEVERAL YEARS. BUT THE TEAM WASN'T ALWAYS A POWERHOUSE.

Oklahoma Agricultural and Mechanical (A&M) was founded in 1890 in Stillwater, Oklahoma. But its first football team, then called the Aggies, wasn't formed until 1901. The Aggies lost their first game 12–0 to nearby Kingfisher College. The program had a slow and rocky start, playing without a coach for their first five years.

Boyd Hill was named the first head coach in 1906. He took over a program that had won only once since 1902. He had a 3–7–2 record for the 1906 season. Paul Davis took the reins in 1909. He led the team for six years. Davis was the program's first winning coach, with a 29–16–1 overall record.

The Davis era included several blowout wins, including a 134–0 defeat of the Phillips University Haymakers on October 3, 1914.

For their first 13 seasons, the Aggies were an independent team. Then A&M joined the one-year-old Southwest Conference in 1915. The Aggies did not win a conference game until the final game of the 1917 season. But it was worth the wait. The Aggies beat the Oklahoma Sooners 9–0.

The game carried greater significance due to a long-standing rivalry with the Sooners. From 1904 to 1918, the Sooners won 12 of 13 games against the Aggies. From 1922 to 1934, the Aggies won five games to Oklahoma's three, with five ties. The rivalry remains strong more than 100 years later. The annual matchup has been nicknamed the "Bedlam" game due to the schools' enthusiastic fans.

John Maulbetsch took over as A&M head coach in 1921. He was still in charge when the school moved to the Missouri Valley Intercollegiate Athletic Association in 1925. Maulbetsch led the Aggies to their first conference title in 1926. The Aggies had a 3–0–1 record in the Missouri Valley, including a 14–14 tie against Oklahoma.

Aggies running back Glen Stafford carries the ball within striking distance of the end zone at the 1945 Cotton Bowl.

In 1928 the conference split to form two new leagues. One was the Big 6, which later became the Big 8 and eventually the Big 12. The other was the Missouri Valley Conference (MVC). The Aggies stuck with the MVC.

Lynn "Pappy" Waldorf led the team to three more MVC championships while coaching from 1929 to 1933. Under Waldorf, the team never lost to Oklahoma. It won three games and tied twice, and its defense shut out the Sooners four straight seasons. With an outstanding record, Waldorf was heavily recruited by other schools, and after the 1933 season he left for Kansas State.

HUMBLE BEGINNINGS

After Waldorf's departure, A&M struggled mightily until Jim Lookabaugh took over as head coach in 1939. Lookabaugh brought stability to the program, guiding the team for 11 years and finishing with an overall record of 58–41–6 in that span.

Under Lookabaugh the Aggies went 8–1 in 1944 to earn their first bowl trip. The team cruised past Texas Christian University 34–0 in the Cotton Bowl. Then, after a narrow 19–14 win against Arkansas to open the 1945 season, the Aggies went on to their first undefeated season in school history.

The season concluded with a 33–13 victory over Saint Mary's in the Sugar Bowl on January 1, 1946. While the Aggies finished with a No. 5 ranking in that season's Associated Press poll, greater laurels were still to come—70 years later. In 2016 the American Football Coaches Association (AFCA) awarded the 1945 national championship to A&M.

An AFCA panel met to determine the winners of the AFCA Coaches' Trophy from 1922, when the association was formed, to 1949, the year before the first coaches' poll was published. Oklahoma State lobbied the panel, pointing out that the 1945 team still held several school records, including a 23.2-point margin of victory. The AFCA determined that A&M deserved to be crowned national champions.

"It is the pleasure of our panel of coaches to officially recognize Oklahoma State's 1945 championship season with the AFCA Coaches' Trophy," AFCA executive director Todd Berry announced.

Lookabaugh coached the Aggies for four more seasons, though none lived up to the success of 1945. A&M won the MVC title in 1948. The Aggies also went to one more bowl under Lookabaugh, losing 20–0 to William & Mary in the Delta Bowl on January 1, 1949.

BOB FENIMORE

Bob Fenimore was one of the first stars of the Oklahoma A&M program. He was known as the "Blond Bomber" during his time in Stillwater. A native of Woodward, Oklahoma, Fenimore set 23 school records as a halfback during his Aggies career. Fenimore led the country in total offense in consecutive seasons. His 1,758 yards from scrimmage were tops in 1944, and he set the pace with 1,641 yards in 1945 for the national champions.

Fenimore was a star on defense too. As of 2017, his 18 career interceptions still stood as a school record. And he also served as the team's punter, posting a 39-yard average in 1945. Fenimore finished third in the Heisman Trophy voting in 1945. Even though a knee injury slowed him as a senior in 1946, the Chicago Bears made him the No. 1 pick of the 1947 NFL Draft. That injury eventually limited him to just 10 games in his NFL career. Fenimore was inducted into the College Football Hall of Fame in 1972.

Cowboys quarterback Scott Burk breaks
down the field in the 1974 Fiesta Bowl.

3

BIG CHANGES

THE POST–WORLD WAR II ERA BROUGHT MANY CHANGES TO THE PROGRAM, INCLUDING A NEW CONFERENCE AND A NEW NAME. THE RENAMED TEAM STRUGGLED TO WIN ON THE FIELD, BUT THESE YEARS SET THE FOUNDATION FOR LATER SUCCESS.

In 1953 the Aggies claimed a share of what would be their final MVC championship. A&M chose to leave the conference in 1956. The team played independently for three years before joining the Big 8 Conference, forerunner to today's Big 12.

Many of the schools on that first Big 8 schedule would become familiar opponents over the next several decades. But those teams would never face an opponent known as Oklahoma A&M, or even the Aggies.

Another change occurred during A&M's independent period. Oklahoma governor Raymond Gary officially changed

The Cowboys' mascot Pistol Pete has a history going back to the 1920s.

the name of the school to Oklahoma State University on May 15, 1957. With a change in name came a change in mascot. Although the football team had been officially named the Aggies, it had gone by a few unofficial names over the years. In the late 1800s and early 1900s, A&M teams played under the name "Tigers." This came from the school calling itself "the Princeton of the Plains," a nod to the highly regarded Ivy League university. OSU's black-and-orange colors trace their roots back to this time.

Sportswriters of the time also referred to the early A&M teams as "Cowpokes" and "Cowpunchers." In 1924 the sports editor of the *Oklahoma City Times* was credited with coining the term "Cowboys" in reference to A&M teams.

The name "Aggies" won out after A&M's athletic department printed up 2,000 balloons with the name "Oklahoma Aggies" on them in 1926. "Aggies" became the officially recognized name of A&M teams for the next three decades.

However, the Cowboys name didn't go away. Many credit this to the legend of Frank B. "Pistol Pete" Eaton. An Oklahoma native and US deputy marshal, Eaton appeared at a parade in the early 1920s with his trademark wide cowboy hat and pistols.

Although the teams were officially called the Aggies, many fans preferred the Cowboys and Cowgirls nicknames. A cartoon image of Pistol Pete helped keep those nicknames fresh in the minds of fans. Finally, in 1957, the school changed names and also renamed the school's teams from Aggies to Cowboys and Cowgirls. In 1984 the school officially adopted the Pistol Pete mascot, too.

BEDLAM

The annual Bedlam game between Oklahoma State and Oklahoma is one of the most heated rivalries in college sports. The competition began between the school's track teams in 1900. The first football game took place in 1904. In 1917 the *Oklahoman* newspaper coined the term "Bedlam" to describe the game's chaotic atmosphere.

Competing as the Cowboys, OSU thrived in its three years as an independent. Head coach Cliff Speegle led his teams to a combined record of 20–10–1 from 1957–59. Speegle led the squad to an 8–3 record in 1958. That season ended with the Cowboys ranked No. 19 in the AP Poll. They went on to defeat Florida State 15–6 in the Bluegrass Bowl.

One of the few down points of the 1958 season was a 7–0 loss to Oklahoma in the annual Bedlam rivalry game. Losing to Oklahoma was common in those days. The Cowboys lost 19 consecutive Bedlam games after their 1945 victory. But fans were given quite a treat for the nearly two-decade wait between wins.

In 1965 the Bedlam game in Norman, Oklahoma, came down to the wire. OSU receiver Lynn Chadwick made a juggling catch, setting up a 35-yard field goal by Charlie Durkee with 1:41 left. The Sooners drove back into Cowboys territory but missed a last-second field goal. The Cowboys won 17–16.

After coming home to Stillwater, the Cowboys found themselves the toast of the town. Players and coaches were treated to free meals in restaurants. The university canceled classes the following Monday.

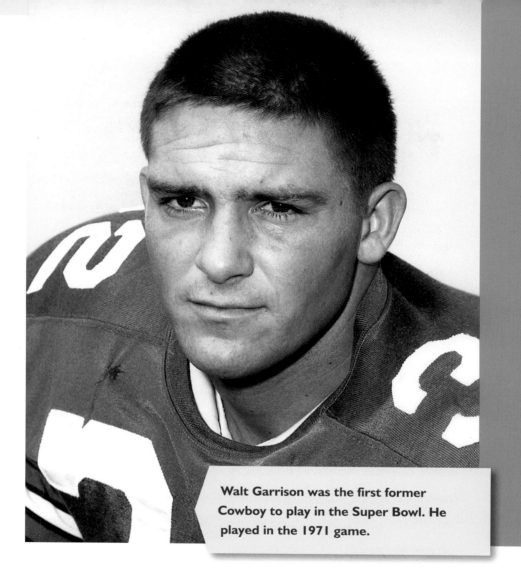

Walt Garrison was the first former Cowboy to play in the Super Bowl. He played in the 1971 game.

In 1966 the Cowboys won again by a lone point, this time on their home field. It all came down to a defensive stop that preserved a 15–14 victory.

Those wins were the last back-to-back Cowboy victories in the Bedlam series until 1997 and 1998. In fact, OSU won only two more Bedlam games in that span. The Cowboys won 31–24 in 1976 and 12–0 in 1995.

JOHN CORKER

John Corker was an All-American linebacker for the Cowboys from 1976 to 1979. Corker became the only OSU player to post at least 100 tackles in each of his four seasons. In 1978 he became the first Cowboy to be honored as Big 8 Defensive Player of the Year. Corker went on to star in the United States Football League (USFL), a rival to the NFL that started play in 1983.

As OSU's Bedlam losses piled up, so did their defeats overall. The Cowboys did not register a winning season from 1960 through 1971. Three coaches came and went until Dave Smith led the team to a 6–5 record in 1972, his only season at the helm. Smith left OSU to coach at Southern Methodist in 1973. But the bit of success he generated in Stillwater continued under coach Jim Stanley.

Stanley took over as head coach after serving as defensive coordinator under Smith the previous season. He led the Cowboys for the next six years. OSU posted winning records in Stanley's first four years. The last coach to do that was Jim Lookabaugh from 1939 to 1942. Stanley also led the Cowboys to their first bowl game in 16 years. The Cowboys beat Brigham Young University (BYU) 16–6 in the 1974 Fiesta Bowl.

The 1976 season stands as the high point of Stanley's time as coach. The Cowboys won the Bedlam game 31–24. The upset over fifth-ranked Oklahoma gave the Cowboys a share of the Big 8 Conference title. The Cowboys finished the season 9–3 after beating BYU again, this time 49–21 in the Tangerine Bowl.

But by 1978, OSU was deep in trouble with the National Collegiate Athletic Association (NCAA). The program was put under probation three times for recruiting violations. Stanley was fired by OSU in 1978 after finishing the season with a 3–8 record. His successor would one day go on to become famous in both college and professional football. But in 1978, he was a rookie head coach just starting out.

His name? Jimmy Johnson.

BIG CHANGES

Running back Thurman Thomas was a star for the Cowboys from 1984–87.

4

SUCCESS AND SANCTIONS

THESE DAYS MOST FOOTBALL FANS KNOW JIMMY JOHNSON AS A TWO-TIME SUPER BOWL–WINNING COACH AND TELEVISION PERSONALITY. BUT IN 1979, HE WAS A ROOKIE HEAD COACH AFTER 15 YEARS AS AN ASSISTANT.

Johnson brought charisma and a winning spirit to a Cowboys program that had fallen on hard times. The 1976 Big 8 Conference title seemed a distant memory. After going 9–3 that year, the Cowboys won seven games *total* in the next two seasons. Couple that with the NCAA sanctions and OSU needed a shot in the arm. Johnson was just the man to provide it.

Johnson led the Cowboys to a 7–4 record in 1979. By 1981 the Cowboys were invited to a bowl game for the first time since 1976. They lost that year's Independence Bowl to Texas A&M, but they were back two years later. The 1983 season set the tone for the rest of the decade, as OSU went

LESLIE O'NEAL

Defensive lineman Leslie O'Neal terrified opposing offenses from 1982 to 1985. A towering presence on the Cowboys' defensive line, O'Neal set a team record with 16.0 sacks in 1984. He was named Big 8 Defensive Player of the Year that season. Through 2017 he was still the school's all-time leader with 34.0 total sacks over his four seasons. O'Neal was an All-American in both 1984 and 1985.

After his time in Stillwater was over, O'Neal went on to a standout career in the NFL. The San Diego Chargers selected him with the eighth overall pick of the 1986 NFL Draft. Only two Cowboys players had ever been drafted that high. After being named the 1986 NFL Defensive Rookie of the Year, he went on to play in six Pro Bowls. He is a member of the Chargers Hall of Fame and the Cowboys Hall of Honor.

8–4 and beat Baylor 24–14 in the Bluebonnet Bowl.

By then Johnson had attracted enough national attention that other schools came calling. He left to take over the program at the University of Miami in June 1984. His friend and assistant coach Pat Jones succeeded Johnson as OSU head coach. He took over a team that had lost just six starters from the previous season.

A 45–3 win at Arizona State in the season opener quickly vaulted OSU to a No. 13 ranking. The Cowboys surged as high as No. 3 at one point, but a Bedlam loss to the second-ranked Sooners dropped them down a couple of notches. Still, OSU finished the season with a 21–14 victory against South Carolina in the Gator Bowl and ended up ranked No. 7 in the nation. That was the Cowboys' highest

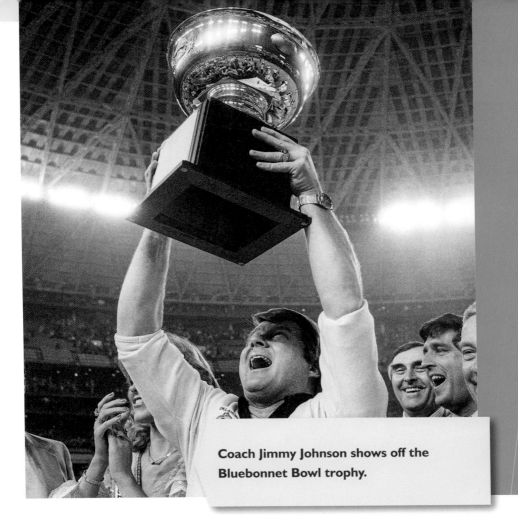

Coach Jimmy Johnson shows off the Bluebonnet Bowl trophy.

year-end ranking since they finished No. 5 after their undefeated season in 1945.

The 1984 season also ushered in a golden era in the OSU backfield. Over the next five years, a pair of future college and Pro Football Hall of Fame running backs ran wild for the Cowboys.

The era began with Thurman Thomas, who came to Stillwater from Houston, Texas. Thomas ran for 843 yards and seven touchdowns that first season, but he exploded in 1985. Thomas ran for 1,650 yards and

15 touchdowns as he helped lead the Cowboys to an 8–4 record and a repeat appearance in the Gator Bowl. He was honored as the Big 8 Offensive Player of the Year.

Thomas's statistics dipped to 741 yards and four touchdowns the next season when he missed some games due to a knee injury. But Thomas's injury gave Cowboys fans an early look at another future Hall of Famer in the backfield—Barry Sanders.

The Wichita, Kansas, native backed up Thomas in 1986, running for 325 yards and two touchdowns while also handling kick and punt returns. The following year, Sanders led college football players by averaging 31.6 yards on kick returns. He also rushed for 603 yards and nine touchdowns while once again backing up Thomas, who had recovered from his injuries.

Back at full strength as a senior, Thomas ran for 1,613 yards and 17 touchdowns. He finished his career as OSU's all-time leading rusher with 5,001 yards and 50 touchdowns. Thomas won his second Big 8 Conference Offensive Player of the Year award and earned All-American honors in 1985. The Cowboys went on to finish 10–2 after a 35–33 win over West Virginia in the Sun Bowl.

But as great as Thomas was in 1987, Sanders topped it with one of the greatest seasons in college history in 1988. With his mentor having been chosen by the Buffalo Bills in the 1988 NFL Draft, Sanders became the Cowboys' starting running back. And he took the ball and ran with it—literally. Sanders rushed for 2,628 yards and 37 touchdowns in 11 games, both NCAA Division I records that remained untouched through 2017.

JASON GILDON

Before going on to an All-Pro career for the Pittsburgh Steelers, Jason Gildon was a feared defender for OSU in the early 1990s. Gildon was a bright spot during one of the darkest times in Cowboys history. The all-time team leader with 63 tackles for loss, Gildon registered three quarterback sacks in one game a school-record five times.

SUCCESS AND SANCTIONS

GERALD HUDSON

Gerald Hudson had the hard task of following Thurman Thomas and Barry Sanders in the OSU backfield. However, Hudson put up two very good seasons as the Cowboys' starting running back after the two future Hall of Famers went on to the NFL. Hudson ran for 910 yards in 1989. He followed it up with 1,642 rushing yards in 1990, earning All-America honors.

Sanders was the runaway winner of the 1988 Heisman Trophy, receiving 559 first place votes. Runner-up Rodney Peete, quarterback for the University of Southern California (USC), received only 70.

But Sanders did not attend the ceremony to pick up his award. Instead, he learned of his win via television while in Tokyo. The Cowboys were in Japan to play in the Coca-Cola Classic against Texas Tech.

OSU won the overseas game 45–42. Then the Cowboys wrapped up their season with a 62–14 win against Wyoming in the Holiday Bowl. Sanders ran for 222 yards and five touchdowns against Wyoming in his final college game.

The Detroit Lions drafted Sanders with the third overall pick of the 1989 NFL Draft. He was not the only Cowboy to depart after the 1988 season. Fellow 1988 All-American wide receiver Hart Lee Dykes also left for the NFL. Dykes had set a Big 8 season record with 1,441 receiving yards. In his time with the Cowboys, he caught 224 passes—many of them thrown by future OSU head coach Mike Gundy. Dykes also posted 3,510 receiving yards and a conference-record 31 touchdown catches.

Bob Simmons led the Cowboys to one bowl game in six years as the OSU head coach.

As much as Dykes helped OSU excel, he was also part of helping bring the Cowboys down. Shortly after the 1988 season ended, the NCAA found OSU guilty of recruiting violations.

The NCAA placed OSU on probation. The school's football games could not be televised for two years, and the Cowboys were banned from bowl games for three years. Head coach Pat Jones was not implicated in the scandal, but the program's reputation suffered. OSU did not win more than four games a season for the rest of Jones's tenure.

Bob Simmons was hired to replace Jones after the 1994 season. Simmons led the Cowboys to an 8–4 record and an appearance in the Alamo Bowl in 1997. But that was Simmons's only winning season with OSU; he retired after a 3–8 season in 2000.

Head coach Les Miles discusses strategy.

5

BOWL BRILLIANCE

AFTER A 20-YEAR ROLLER COASTER OF HIGHS AND LOWS, THE OSU PROGRAM SEEMED TO HAVE MADE NO LASTING PROGRESS. BUT AS THE NEW CENTURY ARRIVED, SO DID ANOTHER CHANGE IN FORTUNES. THE 1990s MARKED ONE OF THE LOWEST PERIODS OF OSU FOOTBALL, WITH JUST ONE WINNING SEASON SINCE 1988. AND AFTER BOB SIMMONS WENT JUST 30–38 OVER SIX SEASONS, IT WAS TIME FOR ANOTHER CHANGE.

Boise State head coach Dirk Koetter was hired in December 2000 to replace Simmons. Just 12 hours later, however, Koetter changed his mind and accepted a position at Arizona State.

OSU had to act quickly to fill the job vacancy. Two candidates remained, and both had strong ties to the program. Les Miles had been OSU's offensive coordinator for three seasons before taking a job with the Dallas Cowboys. Mike Gundy, an assistant coach at Maryland, had played

T. BOONE PICKENS

T. Boone Pickens, an Oklahoma State alumnus, donated $165 million to his alma mater in 2006. It was the largest donation to one program in the history of collegiate athletics. The donation was used to renovate the football stadium that now bears his name. It also helped fund an athletic village for OSU athletes.

quarterback for OSU from 1986 to 1989. Both men were welcomed back to Stillwater. Miles was named head coach, with Gundy as his assistant head coach.

With a new coaching staff in place, Cowboys football also received a major financial boost. Billionaire T. Boone Pickens, an OSU alumnus, began to take an interest in the school's athletic programs. In 2003 Pickens donated $70 million to the school, $20 million of that going toward the football stadium that now bears his name. Three years later he pledged another $165 million to OSU athletics.

Now well funded and with the NCAA sanctions of 1989 a distant memory, OSU football began a steady climb back to respectability. Miles coached the Cowboys to three straight winning seasons starting in 2002. The Cowboys also won consecutive Bedlam games in 2001 and 2002, upsetting Oklahoma teams that were ranked in the top five in the country both years. Miles was chosen as the 2002 Big 12 Conference Coach of the Year.

After the 2004 season Miles left Stillwater for the head coaching job at Louisiana State. The Cowboys handed the keys to Gundy, who had been seen as the head coach in waiting all along.

Alumnus T. Boone Pickens, *left*, and coach Mike Gundy tour the updated stadium.

David Koenig (61) and David Washington (63) protect quarterback Bobby Reid (14) in the 2006 Independence Bowl.

But his head coaching career at OSU had a rocky start, as 11 players were kicked off the team for disciplinary reasons. The Cowboys ended 2005 with a 4–7 record and won just one conference game.

The Cowboys came back strong in the 2006 series, finishing 7–6 with three Big 12 victories. That was the final losing season in conference for the Cowboys until 2014. The 2006 season culminated with Gundy's first bowl game as head coach, a 34–31 defeat of Alabama in the Independence Bowl.

Gundy is one of three Cowboys head coaches to have also played for the team. The other two were Jim Lookabaugh and Floyd Gass. Gundy has directed OSU to the longest period of prosperity in team history.

Through the 2017 season OSU hasn't missed out on a bowl game since Gundy's first season as head coach. In that time, the Cowboys have been regular participants in the big New Year's Day bowl games such as the Cotton Bowl and Sugar Bowl.

One player who helped the Cowboys rise under Gundy was wide receiver Dez Bryant. Before becoming a star in the NFL, Bryant played for OSU from 2007 through 2009. In just over two full seasons, Bryant caught 147 passes for 2,425 yards and 29 touchdowns. He was also named an All-American.

Bryant's college days ended three games into the 2009 season because of an NCAA rule violation regarding contacting an agent. Bryant never played for the Cowboys again. However, his successor, Justin Blackmon, helped carry the team to even greater heights.

NFL DRAFT

Through 2017 a total of 20 Oklahoma State players had been selected in the first round of the NFL Draft, including eight since 2000. Offensive lineman Russell Okung and wide receiver Dez Bryant were selected in the first round in 2010, while wide receiver Justin Blackmon and quarterback Brandon Weeden were first-round picks in 2012. The 2010 draft marked the first time two Cowboys had been selected in the first round since Barry Sanders and Hart Lee Dykes went third and 16th, respectively, in 1989.

BOWL BRILLIANCE

Blackmon was named All-American twice during his three years at OSU. He received the Fred Biletnikoff Award as the nation's top wide receiver twice. From 2009 to 2011, Blackmon caught 253 passes for 3,564 yards and 40 touchdowns. Blackmon caught eight passes for 186 yards and three touchdowns in the Cowboys' Fiesta Bowl win against Stanford.

The 2011 season was a special one in many ways for OSU. The Cowboys attained their highest final Associated Press ranking to date, finishing at No. 3. OSU also won its first Big 12 Conference title that year. The Fiesta Bowl appearance was OSU's first Bowl Championship Series (BCS) game. The top teams in the nation were selected for BCS games from the 1998 to 2013 seasons.

MIKE GUNDY

One of three OSU head coaches to have also played for the team, Mike Gundy is a big part of recent Cowboy history. A native of suburban Oklahoma City, Gundy was named the state's top prep football player in 1986 as a quarterback at Midwest City High School. He turned down an offer from the Oklahoma Sooners to instead play for OSU. He won the Cowboys' starting quarterback job in his freshman year. Gundy went on to become the leading passer in OSU and Big 8 Conference history. In four seasons with the Cowboys, he threw for 7,997 yards and 54 touchdowns.

After his playing days concluded in 1989, Gundy became an assistant coach at OSU. He moved on to Baylor in 1996 and Maryland a year later before returning to OSU as Les Miles's assistant head coach in 2001. Gundy was named the Big 12 Coach of the Year in 2010 and earned the Paul "Bear" Bryant Award as the NCAA Coach of the Year in 2011.

Mike Gundy watches from the sidelines during the 2017 season.

The Cowboys' 8–1 conference record in 2011 included a 44–10 win over Oklahoma. That was OSU's largest margin of victory against the Sooners since 1945. But Oklahoma remains a thorn in the Cowboys' side. Gundy won just two of his first 13 games against the in-state rivals.

Still, the new century has been kind to the orange and black. More than 100 years since its humble beginnings in 1901, OSU has become one of the strongest programs in college football. With teams that are capable of piling up the touchdowns, the Cowboys figure to continue their charge well into their second hundred years.

TIMELINE

The Aggies lose their first game 12–0 to Kingfisher College.

The Aggies lose the first Bedlam game to Oklahoma 75–0 at Island Park in Guthrie on November 5.

Boyd Hill becomes the first Oklahoma A&M football coach.

The Aggies win Bedlam for the first time, 9–0, in Oklahoma City on November 29.

The Aggies win their first conference title in the Missouri Valley with a 3–0–1 conference record.

1901 1904 1906 1917 1926

Bob Fenimore is chosen by the Chicago Bears with the first pick in the NFL Draft.

The Oklahoma A&M Aggies officially become the Oklahoma State Cowboys on May 15.

Oklahoma State joins the Big 8 Conference on June 1.

Dallas Cowboys fullback Walt Garrison becomes the first Oklahoma State alumnus to play in the Super Bowl on January 17.

Jimmy Johnson becomes OSU head coach.

1947 1957 1960 1971 1979

Lynn "Pappy" Waldorf is hired as coach.

Jim Lookabaugh begins 11 years as A&M head coach.

The Aggies win their first bowl title in the Cotton Bowl January 1, beating Texas Christian 34–0.

A&M beats Oklahoma 47–0 in Bedlam November 24 for the greatest margin of victory in a Bedlam game.

The Aggies beat Saint Mary's in the Sugar Bowl 9–0 on January 1.

1929 1939 1945 1945 1946

Pistol Pete, the Cowboys' mascot since the 1920s, is officially approved by OSU.

Barry Sanders becomes the first Heisman Trophy winner in OSU history on December 3.

Mike Gundy becomes OSU head coach on January 3.

The Cowboys win their first outright Big 12 Conference title with a 44–10 win over Oklahoma on December 3.

Oklahoma A&M is retroactively awarded the 1945 Coaches' Trophy national championship on October 13.

1984 1988 2005 2011 2016

QUICK STATS

PROGRAM INFO*
Oklahoma A&M Aggies, 1901–1956
Oklahoma State Cowboys, 1957–

NATIONAL CHAMPIONSHIP
1945

OTHER ACHIEVEMENTS
Big 12 championships: 1
Big 8 championships: 1
Missouri Valley Conference
    championships: 8
Bowl record: 18–10

HEISMAN TROPHY WINNER
Barry Sanders, 1988

KEY COACHES
Mike Gundy (2005–)
    114–53; 8–4 (bowl games)
Jim Lookabaugh (1939–48)
    58–41–6; 2–1 (bowl games)
Lynn "Pappy" Waldorf (1929–33)
    34–10–7

KEY PLAYERS
(POSITION, SEASONS WITH TEAM)
Neill Armstrong (DE/WR, 1943–46)
Justin Blackmon (WR, 2009–11)
Bob Fenimore (HB/DB/P, 1943–46)
Jason Gildon (DE, 1990–93)
Terry Miller (RB, 1974–77)
Mark Moore (S, 1983–86)
Russell Okung (OL, 2006–09)
Leslie O'Neal (DL, 1982–85)
Barry Sanders (RB, 1986–88)
Thurman Thomas (RB, 1984–87)
Brandon Weeden (QB, 2008–11)
Rashaun Woods (WR, 2000–03)

HOME STADIUM
Boone Pickens Stadium (1920–)

*statistics through 2017 season

The first Bedlam game was played November 6, 1904, at Island Park in Guthrie, Oklahoma. At the time, Guthrie was the capital of Oklahoma Territory. The game took place on a cold and windy day. Oklahoma, then known as the Rough Riders, scored a few times when Oklahoma A&M punts blew backwards into the end zone. At one point in the game, the ball rolled into a frozen creek and players from both teams dove in to recover it. The ball was recovered by Oklahoma, which went on to win 75–0.

"We may have been the best team in the country that year. We had a couple of All-Americans and a group of veterans who kept us in check. In practice, we scrimmaged every day. As hard as those scrimmages were, it's a wonder that we had anything left for the games, but those scrimmages toughened us and made us better. We had a lot of older guys who had fought in the war and understood that you don't win anything unless you do it as a team."—Neill Armstrong, Oklahoma A&M All-American, on the undefeated 1945 Aggies. In 2016 the team was retroactively awarded the "Coaches' Trophy" national championship.

The winner of the annual Oklahoma/Oklahoma State Bedlam game takes home a traveling trophy known as the Bedlam Bell. The current trophy is a copy of the original bell clapper from the OSU Old Central building.

GLOSSARY

Aggies
A nickname given to students at an agricultural school or college.

All-American
Designation for players chosen as the best amateurs in the country in a particular sport.

bowl game
A game after the season that teams earn the right to play in by having a good season.

draft
A system that allows teams to acquire new players coming into a league.

implicated
When information is found that shows that a person was involved in something illegal.

mentor
A person who helps teach and tutor a less experienced person.

probation
A period when a person or program is closely watched after breaking the rules.

ranking
A national position as determined by voters.

recruit
To convince a high school player to attend a school in order to play on a sports team.

redshirt
A player who is allowed to practice with a college team but not play in any games for one season.

rival
An opponent with whom a player or team has a fierce and ongoing competition.

upset
An unexpected victory by a supposedly weaker team or player.

FOR MORE INFORMATION

ONLINE RESOURCES

Booklinks
NONFICTION NETWORK
FREE ONLINE NONFICTION RESOURCES

To learn more about the Oklahoma State Cowboys, visit abdobooklinks.com.
These links are routinely monitored and updated to provide the most current
information available.

BOOKS

Allen, Robert. *More Than a Championship: The 2011 Oklahoma State Cowboys.*
  Oklahoma City, OK: Oklahoma Heritage Association, 2012.

Kovacs, Vic. *Touchdown! The History of Football.* New York: Crabtree
  Publishing, 2016.

Wilner, Barry. *The Story of the Fiesta Bowl.* Minneapolis, MN: Abdo
  Publishing, 2016.

PLACES TO VISIT

Boone Pickens Stadium
700 West Hall of Fame Avenue
Stillwater, OK 74075
877-255-4678
www.okstate.com/sports/2015/6/18/GEN_0618155302.aspx

Originally known as Lewis Field, Boone Pickens Stadium has been home to Cowboys
football since 1913. It is the oldest football stadium in the Big 12 Conference and
underwent extensive remodeling beginning in 2003.

INDEX

ABOUT THE AUTHOR

Thomas Carothers has been a sportswriter for the past 15 years in the Minneapolis/St. Paul, Minnesota, area. He has worked for a number of print and online publications, mostly focusing on prep sports coverage. He lives in Minneapolis with his wife and a house full of dogs.